Superb Social Skills
in the primary classroom

Book 1

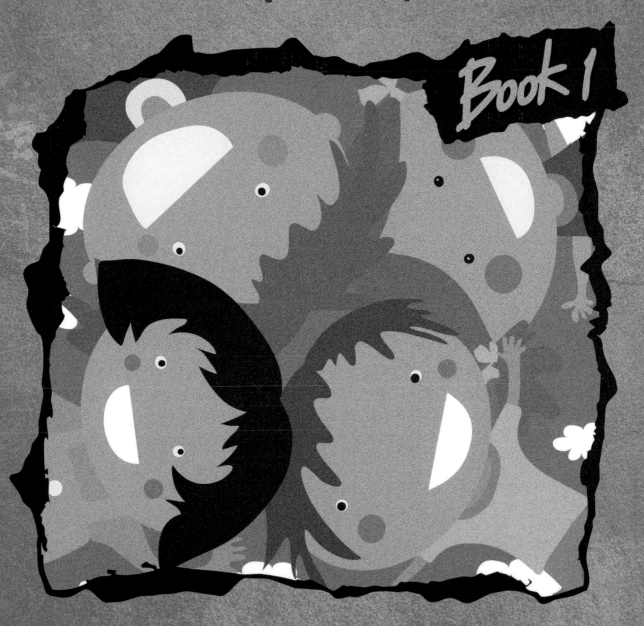

Janet Bruce

Title:	Superb Social Skills in The Primary Classroom Book 1
Author:	Janet Bruce
Designer:	Delineate Ltd
Editor:	Tanya Tremewan
Book code:	PB00135
ISBN:	978-1-908736-14-7
Published:	2012
Publisher:	TTS Group Ltd
	Park Lane Business Park Kirkby-in-Ashfield Notts, NG17 9GU Tel: 0800 318 686 Fax: 0800 137 525
Websites:	www.tts-shopping.com
Copyright:	Text: © Janet Bruce, 2009 Edition and Illustrations: © TTS Group Ltd, 2012
About the author:	Janet Bruce has a major in inclusive education. She has taught at all levels of primary school in Australia, including children with special needs. As coordinator of the Schools Student Welfare Support Group, she facilitated group discussions between parents and teachers of children experiencing various social difficulties, in order to come up with achievable goals and practical ideas to assist these children. The support material and activities in this series have been developed through her work with various children requiring further social skill support and have been used successfully with them.

Photocopy Notice:

Permission is given to schools and teachers who buy this book to reproduce it (and/or any extracts) by photocopying or otherwise, but only for use at their present school. Copies may not be supplied to anyone else or made or used for any other purpose.

Contents

Introduction	4	**Social stories**	34

Introduction   4
Navigating your way
through this book

Friendship   6
Friendship skills
Asking to join in
Lunch time play
Solving conflict
Role play

Making decisions   12
Taking turns game
Choosing games
Saying "No"

Me and my self-esteem   17
Emotions on my face
Feeling happy
Feeling sad
Feeling excited
Feeling angry
When I feel …
Pictures for my feelings
Angry action plan

Social skills   27
Greeting people
Talking to friends
What does it look like
to be a good listener?
Listening and responding
When is it appropriate?
Looking people in the eye

Social stories   34
My story of listening in class
My story of having a
different teacher
My story of school assembly
My lunch time story
My story of a class trip

School life skills   40
Money
Healthy choices
Following instructions
In an emergency
Getting organised

Routines   46
Before school routine
Getting ready to go
to the library
Packing up to go home
Time to do my work

Timetables   50
Daily timetable
Weekly timetable
Term timetable
Play timetable
Weekend timetable

Introduction

This *Superb Social Skills in The Primary Classroom* series aims to encourage critical social skills in children from 5 to 10 years of age. Its activities provide children with structured learning opportunities to play and practise social skills they have learnt. Their purpose is to assist children to develop more sophisticated social strategies and maintain stable relationships with other children and adults.

As teachers know, there are many children within every classroom who require further support and instruction on use of appropriate social skills. Included within this group are those with special needs. Although social skills do not receive the same attention as academic skills in the classroom, in many ways they are just as important for success.

It is helpful for special needs children and others requiring further social skills training to learn how to think about relationships and the consequences of their actions. They often need to be given direct, explicit instructions about how to behave in specific social situations. For example, a child may need to be told that it is important to say, "Hello" when somebody greets them, or to smile when asking a child to join in a game. Learning these skills is not easy, and most children need to be told the same information many times before they learn them fully. Therefore the range of activities in this series covers broad topics to teach and reinforce these skills and understandings.

Navigating your way through this book

This book for ages 5 to 7 years begins with five sections designed to help children in this age group to explore the issues related to social skills and become successful in their social interactions with their peers. The first four of these sections are activity based and cover:

- friendship
- making decisions
- me and my self-esteem
- social skills.

The fifth section contains social stories that assist in making children more aware of others and how they should behave in social situations.

The final three sections offer additional activities and resources for children with greater needs. They deal with:

- school life skills
- routines
- timetables.

In combination the activities encourage children to develop resilient, positive attitudes and to think about appropriate actions and responses in social situations. As they are supported to succeed in many different social situations and develop stronger relationships, they will, in turn, learn how to take a positive view of others and themselves as playmates.

Friendship

Everybody needs friends around them. Friends are there to share the good times and the bad times. Establishing strong friendships is a key part of a child's social development. A child can feel sad and lonely without someone to play with, talk to and share their experiences with.

In interacting with friends, children learn many social skills, such as how to communicate, cooperate and solve problems. They develop the ability to think through and talk about different situations in their relationships. They practise dealing with their emotions and responding to the emotions of others. Moreover, when children have friends at school they generally also have more positive attitudes towards school and learning.

Knowing how to treat people is an important skill. Once a child makes a new friend they will need the skills and knowledge to maintain a healthy relationship as well.

The activities in this section help children to make and maintain healthy friendships. Through completing the activities children will come to understand that in order to have friends they need to be a good friend themselves.

> *The activities ahead ...*
>
> **Friendship skills.** Children reflect on the characteristics of a good friend.
>
> **Asking to join in.** Children envisage themselves in a range of situations where they might approach their peers to see if they can join in with a game.
>
> **Lunch time play.** Children set out specific options open to them for playing in the lunch break.
>
> **Solving conflict.** Children learn four essential steps for dealing constructively with conflict.
>
> **Role play.** Children play charades based on a range of social scenarios.

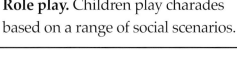

Friendship skills

Circle all of the characteristics that make a **good** friend.

*To have good friends you must **be** a good friend!*

- Listening to each other
- Hurting each other's feelings
- Teasing each other
- Helping each other solve problems
- Giving each other compliments
- Being reliable
- Understanding each other's feelings and moods
- Hurting each other
- Respecting each other
- Being honest with each other
- Lying to each other
- Caring about each other
- Using nice manners with each other
- Yelling at each other
- Having fun together
- Being bossy

© TTS Group Ltd, 2012

Asking to join in

Suppose some other children were playing these games. How could you ask to join in with them? Write what you would do or say under each one.

When you find that you don't have anyone to play with, you can ask to join in other people's games.

Playing hopscotch _____

_____

_____

Playing soccer (football) _____

_____

_____

Playing handball _____

_____

_____

Playing skipping _____

_____

_____

What is another game or activity that you like to do?

_____

Write how you could ask to join in with it.

_____

_____

_____

© TTS Group Ltd, 2012

Lunch time play

What can you do at lunch time today? What are your options? Write your ideas in the chart.

At lunch time I can organise an activity and ask others to join in my game or I can ask to join in with someone else's game.

I can organise to play …	I can ask to play …

© TTS Group Ltd, 2012

Solving conflict

Sometimes we can get pretty angry or feel that something is unfair. So what should we do? We could throw a huge tantrum or we could try to sort things out.

Here are a few things that you need to do to sort out the problem.

1. **Stop** before you lose your temper.

2. **Say** what is bothering you.

3. **Listen** to the other person.

4. **Think** of a solution to the problem that will satisfy everyone.

Write down the four steps for solving a conflict in the stepping stones.

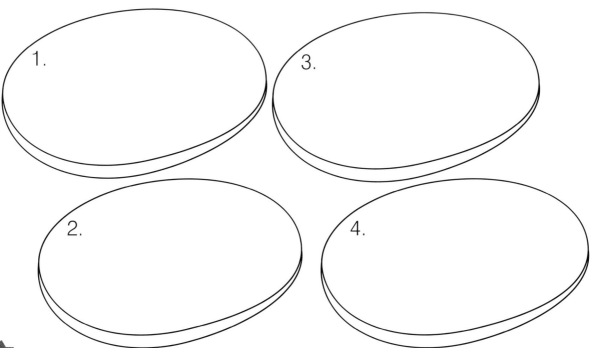

Role play

Instructions for the teacher

Complete this activity with a small group of children.

1. Cut out each action listed below and place all the strips in a hat or box.

2. Ask each child to choose a strip of paper from the hat and act it out **without** using their voice. The other members of the group try to guess the action.

I just love to act out different things without using words. This is called **playing charades**.

Asking to join in a game of soccer (football)

Ignoring someone who is teasing you

Saying hello to a friend who is way across the playground

Arguing with a friend about the choice of game

Saying you are sorry

Forgiving a friend and making up after a fight

Laughing at a funny joke your friend shared with you

Receiving a present and a card from your friend

Playing your favourite game with your best friend

Making decisions

Making decisions can be a hard task for children especially when they need to consider others' wishes and opinions. Children don't always know what to do when they must make a complex decision.

On a daily basis, for example, children face the challenge of deciding what activity they will play with their friends. When each party wants to play something different, conflict often arises.

The activities in this section teach children about the importance of making fair decisions and strengthen the skills that they need when playing with others. Children will:

- gain confidence with negotiating and compromising to make fair joint decisions
- explore and be made aware of others' feelings
- learn about saying "No" as a good, safe choice.

The activities ahead ...

- **Taking turns game.** Children play a board game with an emphasis on turn-taking.

- **Choosing games.** Children work through a positive way of deciding what game to play when they and their friends disagree about which one to play.

- **Saying "No".** Children learn four basic steps to take when it is a safe, healthy response to say "No" to a friend's idea.

Taking turns game

To play this game, you will need a counter for each player and one dice.

Special rule! If you try to roll the dice before it is your turn, you must go back to the start.

How to play

1. Roll the dice to see who will start. The player with the highest number has the first turn.

2. Take turns to roll the dice and move your counter along.

3. The first player to reach the end is the winner if they can say one reason why it is good to take turns.

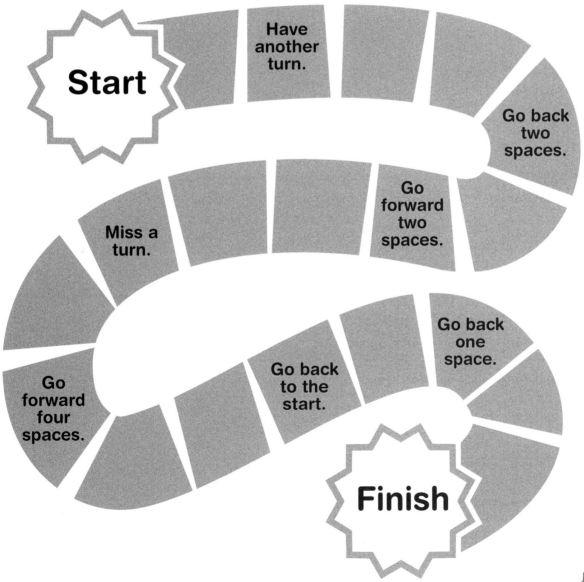

Choosing games

It is fun to play games with friends. So it is good if everyone agrees on what to play.

Sometimes it is hard for my friends and me to agree on what we should play. We always try really hard to work it out nicely.

How can we decide together what to play?

1. First we **listen** to each other's ideas.

2. Then we try to **compromise** and come to a decision.

3. If we can't decide on one game, we can **take turns** to play different games so that everyone plays what they want to.

Write the three steps for choosing a game in the stairs. Use your own words if you don't want to write all of the words used above.

What do you do?

Write your answers to these questions.

What games do you like to play?

_____

_____

What games do other children like to play?

_____

_____

How do you usually decide what to play?

_____

_____

What will you do when you are finding it hard to make a decision about what to play next time?

_____

_____

Draw a picture of you and your friends working out what game to play.

Saying "No"

If your friend suggests doing something bad or dangerous, then look your friend straight in the eye and confidently say, "No". Here is what to say and do next.

Saying "No" can be really hard but sometimes it is a really good, safe thing to do.

1. **Name the problem.** Say, "That's dangerous" or "That's mean".

   That is dangerous

2. **Say what could happen.** It might be that you could get hurt, you could get into trouble or you could feel bad if you did the wrong thing. Tell your friend which of these problems is bothering you.

3. **Suggest something else to do.** Having another suggestion makes it easier for your friend to go along with you.

   How about we try to build the biggest Lego tower ever?

4. If you can't change your friend's mind, **walk away** but let your friend know he or she is welcome to join you.

   I'm going inside to start building the tower. If you change your mind, come in and help me.

Me and my self-esteem

Imagine how life would be if you were unable to name any of your emotional states. The ability to name a feeling is the first step towards being able to manage it. If children can identify when they are angry, then they can apply the strategies they know for dealing with anger, such as walking away, taking a drink of water or breathing deeply. Without a name for the feeling, it is much harder to decide on a correct course of action.

Therefore children need to be taught an emotional vocabulary in order to begin to learn the complex skills of regulating and communicating about emotions. The simplest emotional vocabulary covers the four fundamental human emotions:

- *happy* (joyous, peaceful, content)
- *sad* (down, blue, gloomy)
- *excited* (thrilled, upbeat, energised)
- *angry* (irritable, furious, mad).

Children readily understand the terms *happy*, *sad*, *excited* and *angry* and can use them to label their emotions. Identifying emotions with these terms can also become the basis for teaching children basic skills of emotional regulation.

An easy way to teach an emotional vocabulary to children is through emoticons – simple icons of faces expressing a particular emotion. Without a developed emotional vocabulary, young children can point to a face that expresses how they are feeling. They can then learn to associate this picture with the appropriate word.

Part of teaching children an affective vocabulary is to teach them that all emotions are okay but that some of the ways we act out those emotions may not be. Emotional self-acceptance begins with adults who genuinely accept the feelings that a child experiences and teaches them how to regulate their emotions.

The activities in this section help children to understand their emotions and deal with them successfully.

The activities ahead …

- **Emotions on my face.** Children identify typical times when they become happy, sad, angry or excited, and relate these feelings to a particular facial expression.

- **Feeling happy.** Children identify the causes of happiness.

- **Feeling sad.** Children identify the causes of sadness and ways of overcoming it.

- **Feeling excited.** Children identify the causes of excitement and consider why certain experiences do or do not excite them.

- **Feeling angry.** Children consider how their body responds when they feel angry.

- **When I feel …** Children explore appropriate ways of behaving when they feel happy, sad, angry or excited.

- **Pictures for my feelings.** Use this wide range of emoticons to teach about feelings in a variety of ways.

- **Angry action plan.** Children identify specific steps they can take to work through an experience of anger.

Emotions on my face

What do the faces show?

Look carefully at the expression on each face below. Choose one word from the box that names the feeling that the face shows. Then write the word on the line under the face.

We can tell a lot about how a person is feeling by the expression on their face.

| Sad | Excited |
| Angry | Happy |

_____ _____ _____ _____

When do you feel …?

What might have happened to the person to make them have each of these feelings? Talk about it with a partner or with your class. Then write your ideas below.

I feel happy when _____
_____

 I feel sad when _____
_____

 I feel excited when _____
_____

 I feel angry when _____
_____

Feeling happy

Draw your happy face on this picture.

I am so cheerful and full of life when I am feeling happy.

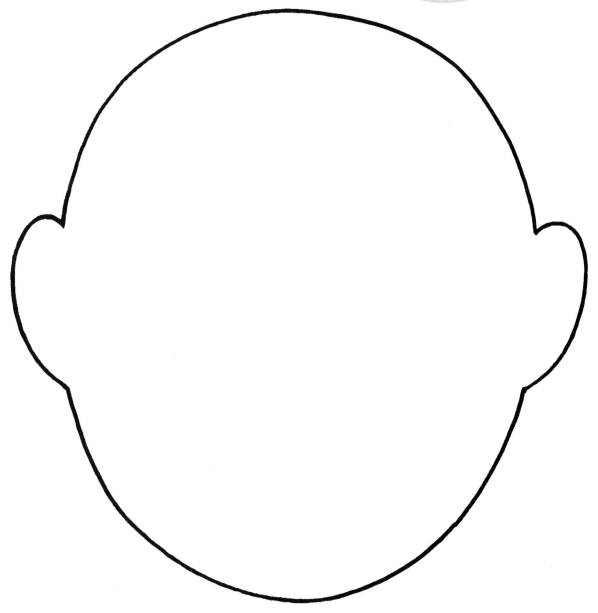

What sort of things make you feel happy? Draw these things around the face and label each one.

Feeling sad

Think of a time when you felt **sad**. Draw a picture of what your face looks like when you feel sad.

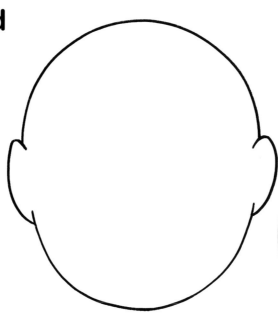

Feeling sad is OK! We all feel blue from time to time.

What happened to make you feel sad?

_____

_____

Why do you think you feel better now about whatever made you sad?

_____

_____

Over time the feeling of sadness goes away and you begin to feel better and better.

_____

When you feel sad or blue next time, you can cheer yourself up by:

- _____
- _____
- _____

Feeling excited

Put a circle around the things below that make you feel **excited**.

*I am so **excited**! There are only three more days until it's my birthday.*

Doing your homework

Your birthday party

Opening presents on Christmas morning

Going fishing

Cleaning your room

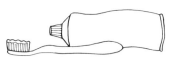

Brushing your teeth

Going to the zoo

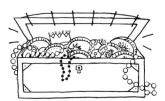

Finding treasure

Discuss these questions with a partner or your class:

- Why do you get excited about the things you circled?
- Why do you **not** get excited about the things you did **not** circle?

Feeling angry

Think of a time when you felt **angry** about something. What did you notice happened to your body when you became angry? Show what happened on the picture below and label the different parts of your drawing.

When I get angry I stamp my feet, clench my fists and raise my voice.

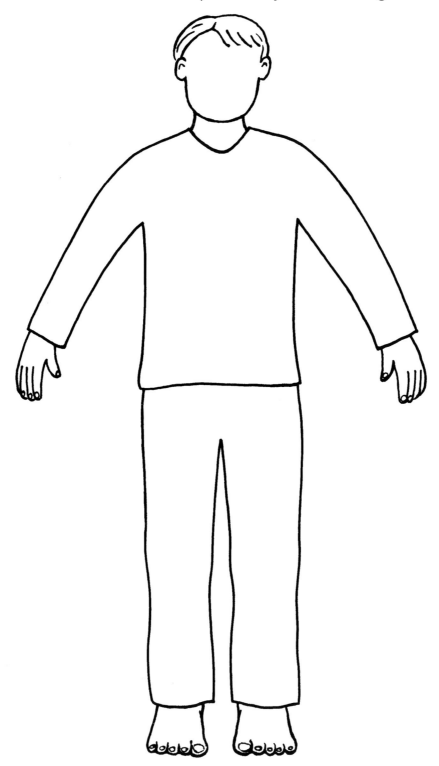

When I feel ...

List some appropriate things to do when you have each feeling below.

> *Sometimes it is hard to know the right thing to do when I am feeling happy, sad, excited or angry.*

When I feel **happy**, I can _____

_____

_____

_____

When I feel **sad**, I can _____

_____

_____

_____

When I feel **excited**, I can _____

_____

_____

_____

When I feel **angry**, I can _____

_____

_____

_____

Tick one idea for each feeling that you think you might try next time you feel that way.

Pictures for my feelings

Angry action plan

Sometimes I can get **angry**.

Here is what I can do if I start to feel angry.

First I can _____

_____

_____

Then I can _____

_____

_____

Then I can _____

_____

_____

Then I can _____

_____

_____

Then I can _____

_____

_____

Then I will feel better.

Social skills

Social skills are a central part of life. Wherever we go we are constantly interacting with others. We are meeting and greeting people, participating in conversations, listening to others and responding when appropriate.

Taking part in these kinds of interactions can be incredibly difficult for some children. Therefore it is important to explicitly teach these skills so that they can confidently communicate and interact with others.

The activities in this section deal specifically with the social skills that we all need to participate and communicate effectively in society. In completing them children will develop the confidence to use the appropriate skills in real life situations.

The activities have been designed particularly to assist children with special needs and other children requiring additional support with their social skills.

> *The activities ahead ...*
>
> - **Greeting people.** Children visualise a variety of situations when a greeting is appropriate and propose an appropriate response (in actions and words) for each one.
>
> - **Talking to friends.** Children come up with some ways to open a conversation with a friend in different situations.
>
> - **What does it look like to be a good listener?** Children use a picture to show the body language of someone who is listening well.
>
> - **Listening and responding.** In pairs children practise the body language of good listening.
>
> - **When is it appropriate?** Children identify appropriate behaviour from a range of options.
>
> - **Looking people in the eye.** Children learn about the importance of making eye contact.

© TTS Group Ltd, 2012

Greeting people

There are many different ways we can greet people.

Decide what would be a good thing to do and say to greet people in each of these situations.

1. When an adult passes me in the corridor …

    I can say _____

    I can *(action)* _____

2. When a classmate stands next to me in line …

    I can say _____

    I can *(action)* _____

3. When someone knocks on the door at home …

    I can say _____

    I can *(action)* _____

4. When I want to ask to join in with a game …

    I can say _____

    I can *(action)* _____

5. When I meet a new classmate for the first time …

    I can say _____

    I can *(action)* _____

Talking to friends

Look at each picture below and write down what you would say in that situation.

I would really like to play with Scott.

I can say _____

_____

_____

I would like to talk to Jenny.

I can say _____

_____

_____

I would love to ask to join in with their game.

I can say _____

_____

_____

I would love to play handball with Sam.

I can say _____

_____

_____

What does it look like to be a good listener?

Label the person below to show what a good listener does with their body when they are being a good listener.

When you are a good listener, you pay attention to what the person is saying and you show them that you are paying attention.

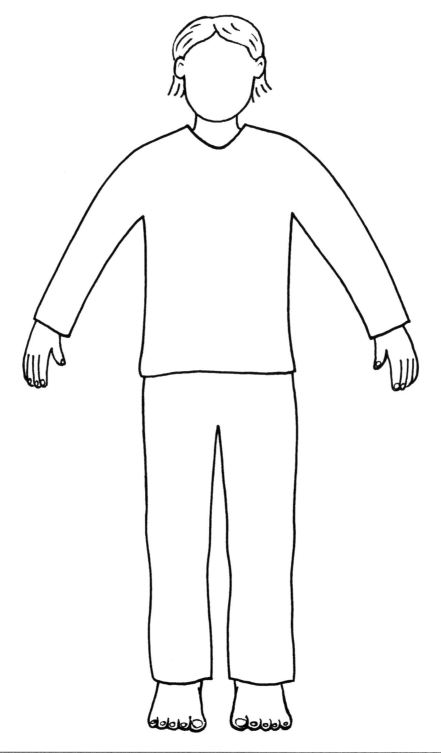

Listening and responding

Do you know all the ways to show you are a good listener?

When I am listening to others speak, I show that I am being a good listener in all these ways:

- I look at the person.
- I make eye contact.
- I move my head.
- I show expression on my face.
- I wait my turn to speak.
- I keep my hands and body still.
- I respond by asking a question or making a comment when they have finished.
- I show interest in what the person is saying.

1. Write about all of the different things you did this morning to get ready for school.

   _____

   _____

   _____

   _____

2. Working in a pair, listen to your partner as they speak about what they did to get ready for school. Your job is to show you are being a good listener by doing everything listed in the box above while you are listening.

When is it appropriate?

Circle Yes or No for each possible answer.

*Appropriate is another way of saying **OK**.*

1. When is it appropriate to say "Hello" to someone?
   a. When you meet a friend — Yes / No
   b. When you are walking through a crowd of people — Yes / No
   c. When you pass a stranger on the street — Yes / No

2. When is it appropriate to yell or use a loud voice?
   a. When you are in the classroom — Yes / No
   b. When you are playing outside — Yes / No
   c. When you are sitting next to a classmate in assembly — Yes / No

3. When is it appropriate to hug someone?
   a. When someone smiles at you — Yes / No
   b. When you see your teacher — Yes / No
   c. When your friend has hurt themselves — Yes / No

4. When is it appropriate to talk to other children at school?
   a. When you are in assembly — Yes / No
   b. When the teacher says it is OK to talk — Yes / No
   c. When you are at your desk doing work — Yes / No

5. When is it appropriate to play?
   a. When you are supposed to be working — Yes / No
   b. When it is lunch time — Yes / No
   c. When you have finished your work — Yes / No

Looking people in the eye

Draw the eyes on the head below. Then use this picture to practise making eye contact.

> *When we talk to someone or when someone speaks to us, it is polite to look the person in the eye.*

Social stories

A social story is a vignette that briefly describes a particular social skill or a crucial concept to do with a social situation. The goal of a social story is to teach social skills in a way that the child understands easily.

A social story provides children with a number of strategies to learn how to respond or behave in that situation. It can help them make sense of everyday events and provide cues and strategies to inform children how to behave appropriately.

As well as teaching new social skills, a social story reinforces behaviours and skills that children have already acquired. It guides them to make the right choices when they are in particular situations.

This section offers social stories for a range of school-based situations. In some stories children are actively involved by filling in missing words.

The social stories ahead ...

- My story of listening in class
- My story of having a different teacher
- My story of school assembly
- My lunch time story
- My story of a class trip

My story of listening in class

My name is _____

I am in Year _____ at _____ School.

My teacher's name is _____

In my classroom, we sit at our desks to do our work.

Sometimes we sit on the floor and listen to the teacher.

When the teacher is talking to the class, I try to be quiet and listen carefully.

When I want to say something or answer a question, I put my hand up and wait for the teacher to say my name.

When the teacher says my name, I know that it is my turn to speak.

The teacher will be very happy if I listen and put my hand up to speak.

My story of having a different teacher

My teacher is called _____

On some days, my teacher is away.

Sometimes the reason for being away is that _____ is ill.

Other times _____ might be away learning new things.

On those days, I will have a different teacher.

I will treat my new teacher like I treat my usual teacher, _____

I will follow our class rules and do my best work while my teacher is away.

Then _____ will come back to school.

My teacher will be happy that I have been trying hard to do my best work.

I will tell _____ about the things that I have learnt while the different teacher was here.

My story of school assembly

Sometimes we have assemblies at school.

When it is time to go, my teacher will walk me to assembly.

My teacher will show me where to sit.

There are a lot of other children there.

When I go to assembly, I will sit still and listen to the person speaking.

I will clap when everyone else claps.

When I go to assembly, I will try to watch what the other children are doing and to listen to my teacher.

When children are performing, it is polite to watch quietly.

If I sit still and listen in assembly, my teacher will be very proud of me.

My lunch time story

At lunch time I can go outside to play after I have eaten my lunch.

I can walk around and play games.

I can also talk out loud.

I always stay in the playground where the teacher can see me.

When I go outside, I can move around.

I can run, hop, skip and walk.

I can choose the games that I want to play.

I like playing with my friends sometimes. At other times I like to play on my own.

When lunch time is over, I need to line up and go back to my classroom.

When I am in my class, I will feel ready to sit down quietly again.

I will sit at my desk, read a book and be quiet.

My story of a class trip

Sometimes our class goes on trips.

I look forward to our class trips because we go to special places.

My teacher talks to us about the class trip before we leave.

I get a special note about the class trip to show Mum or Dad.

Mum or Dad has to sign the note. Then I have to give it back to my teacher.

When it is time to go on the class trip, we get on a bus.

I start to get excited when I am on the bus because I know we are going somewhere new and exciting.

When I am on the class trip, I must always stay with my teacher so that I don't get lost.

Sometimes I feel very excited when I am on the class trip.

When we have finished our class trip, we get on the bus to go back to school.

School life skills

To succeed and become independent within the school setting, children must master a number of important skills related to school life. Concentrating, regulating one's own behaviour and being organised, for example, are skills that many children struggle with. Yet these skills are essential if children are to achieve academic success and become integrated into the classroom and school life. Being able to follow instructions and show some level of organisation will assist children greatly at school.

In addition, children need to use and understand money so that they can order and purchase food from the school canteen or tuck shop. They need to be able to think laterally to solve little problems as they arise throughout each day, and seek alternative solutions.

The activities in this section offer explicit teaching and learning opportunities for children to gain knowledge of and confidence with all of these skills. Through completing the activities, children who require additional support will come to understand what to do in a range of situations at school. With their greater understanding of how to do particular tasks, they will in turn develop greater independence and confidence at school.

> *The activities ahead ...*
>
> - **Money.** Children identify the amount of money they need, and how much this looks like in coins, for the tuck shop food they like.
> - **Healthy choices.** Children distinguish between the healthy foods and the unhealthy foods that they like from the tuck shop.
> - **Following instructions.** Children practise creating their own lunch order, following all the necessary steps.
> - **In an emergency.** Children identify safe, effective ways of acting in a range of different emergencies.
> - **Getting organised.** Children work out how to lay out their belongings in their desk in an organised, readily useable way.

Money

What sort of things do you like to buy from the school tuck shop?

I love it when I can buy myself a treat from the school tuck shop.

In the first column of the table below, list the tuck shop foods you like. Then find out how much each one costs and write the amount in the middle column. In the last column, draw or create a rubbing of the coins you need to buy the food.

Food	How much does it cost?	What coins do you need?

Healthy choices

What **healthy** foods do you like to buy at the tuck shop?

What **unhealthy** foods do you like to buy at the tuck shop?

Write your answers in the chart.

I am so glad I can buy yummy things from the school tuck shop. There are some yummy, healthy foods that are really good for us to eat. But some foods at the tuck shop are unhealthy, and we should only eat them sometimes.

Healthy foods	Unhealthy foods

Following instructions

Follow these instructions to write your very own lunch order.

> If your school deals with lunch orders in a different way, find out more about it with your teacher and try writing instructions together for someone else to follow.

1. Find a menu from your school canteen or tuck shop.
2. Read the items you can choose from the menu. What will you choose?
3. Write your name and class on the lunch order bag or envelope.
4. Write what you will order. Write how much each item costs too.
5. Add up the cost of all of the food you have ordered and write this total.
6. Write down how much money you have put in the bag or envelope.
7. Will you get change? If so, write down how much change you will receive.
8. Place your money inside the lunch order bag or envelope.
9. Fold over the lunch order bag or stick down the envelope so that your money won't fall out.
10. Take your order to the school office or to the canteen or tuck shop.

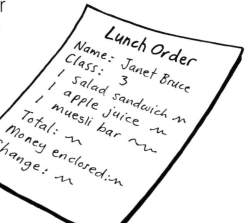

In an emergency

Read the stories below. For each one, think about what you need to do to help yourself or another person. Write your answer on the lines.

When it's an emergency, you can help best if you know what to do and if you act quickly.

One of the youngest children at school falls over and hits their head on the concrete during lunch time. How can you help?

_____

_____

You find a needle in the garden at school. What should you do?

_____

_____

You accidentally cut your finger with a pair of scissors. What should you do?

_____

_____

You see a big, fierce-looking dog in the playground. What should you do?

_____

_____

You see some bigger kids pushing around another kid in the playground. How can you help?

_____

_____

Getting organised

Cut out the items below. Then arrange them in the desk below. Try to arrange the items so that you can use and put away everything in it easily.

When I store my belongings in an organised way, it is easier to work and find the things I need.

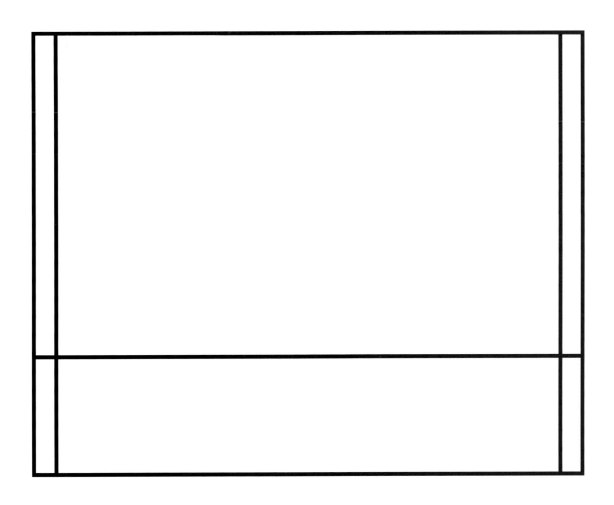

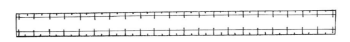

Routines

Routines play a vital role in creating happy, relaxed children. Daily routines provide the vital cues that indicate change and order within the day. For example, the routine of brushing teeth in the evening sends a message to the child that bed time is coming next.

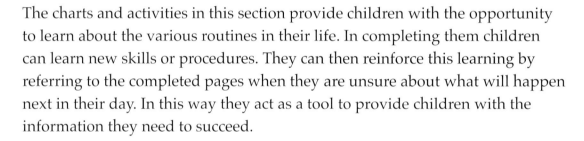

Children who have consistent routines develop a strong connection with them and are able to predict what happens in their day. An organised and predictable environment helps children feel safe and secure. Therefore maintaining normal daily routines as much as possible can make it easier for children to cope with change and deal with stress.

The charts and activities in this section provide children with the opportunity to learn about the various routines in their life. In completing them children can learn new skills or procedures. They can then reinforce this learning by referring to the completed pages when they are unsure about what will happen next in their day. In this way they act as a tool to provide children with the information they need to succeed.

Although routines take effort to set up and maintain, once established they help the child to behave automatically in many areas. The activities in this section assist with the process of setting up individual routines with children for different purposes. They are also a great resource for reinforcing expectations about procedures and routines while at school.

> *The activities ahead ...*
>
> - **Before school routine.** Children draw a comic strip of all the things they need to do at home to get ready for going to school.
>
> - **Getting ready to go to the library.** Children draw a comic strip of their preparations for going to the school library.
>
> - **Packing up to go home.** Children draw a comic strip showing the routine at the end of the school day.
>
> - **Time to do my work.** Children identify actions they can take to settle down to work.

Before school routine

Draw a comic strip that shows what you do every morning to get ready for school. Use speech bubbles to show some things that you and others in your family say.

When I get ready to go to school, I have to ….

There's a lot to do before school – but it helps to know it's usually the same things every day.

© TTS Group Ltd, 2012

Getting ready to go to the library

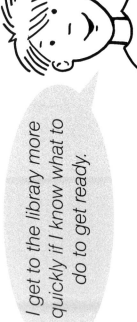

I get to the library more quickly if I know what to do to get ready.

What steps do you need to take to get ready to go to the school library? Draw a comic strip that shows these steps.

Packing up to go home

What steps do you need to take to get ready to go home at the end of the school day? Draw a comic strip that shows these steps.

Time to do my work

When it is time to do work at my desk, I need to remember to …

There are things I can do to help myself settle down to my work and work well.

1. _____

2. _____

3. _____

4. _____

5. _____

Then I can work really well.

Timetables

Understanding and following an individual timetable can be a way for an anxious child to find predictability and confidence. The timetables in this section can be copied and altered to reflect an individual child's routine. The following five types of timetables are included.

Daily timetable

Fill in the daily timetable with the activities the child does every day. The child then ticks each one off as they achieve it, gaining a sense of satisfaction along with specific information about what they can expect to do in their day.

Weekly timetable

Fill in the weekly timetable with subjects or activities for the week ahead. The child can then gain a sense of satisfaction in ticking off each activity as they complete it and a feeling of predictability about what will happen during the week.

Term timetable

Fill in the term timetable with important events such as a swimming carnival, special performances and field trips. From this timetable the child can identify when a special event is going to take place, count down to the event and be reminded that a special day is approaching.

Play timetable

The play timetable can be a useful tool for children who need to plan their play activities during the breaks in the school day. It is particularly helpful for children who require a little more structure.

Weekend timetable

The weekend timetable can be useful for children who have a busy weekend schedule. It can be used to plan out their activities and help to structure a weekend.

Daily timetable

Today is _____   Date: _____

Activity	Finished
Play	
Play	

Weekly timetable

Week: _____ Term: _____

Monday	Finished	Tuesday	Finished	Wednesday	Finished	Thursday	Finished	Friday	Finished

Term timetable

Term: _____ Year: _____

Week	Monday	Tuesday	Wednesday	Thursday	Friday
1					
2					
3					
4					
5					
6					
7					
8					
9					
10					

Play timetable

	Monday	Tuesday	Wednesday	Thursday	Friday
Before school					
Recess/ break					
Lunch					

Weekend timetable

Time	Saturday	Time	Sunday